W9-CFK-994

Distinctions in Nature

Insects and Arachnids Explained

Laura L. Sullivan

Cavendish Square

New York

Published in 2017 by Cavendish Square Publishing, LLC
243 5th Avenue, Suite 136, New York, NY 10016

Copyright © 2017 by Cavendish Square Publishing, LLC

First Edition

Library of Congress Cataloging-in-Publication Data

Names: Sullivan, Laura L.
Title: Insects and arachnids explained / Laura L. Sullivan.
Description: New York : Cavendish Square Publishing, 2017. | Series: Distinctions in nature | Includes index.
Identifiers: ISBN 9781502621894 (pbk.) | ISBN 9781502622662 (library bound) |
ISBN 9781502621900 (6 pack) | ISBN 9781502621917 (ebook)
Subjects: LCSH: Insects—Juvenile literature. | Arachnida—Juvenile literature.
Classification: LCC QL467.2 S85 2017 | DDC 595.7—dc23

Editorial Director: David McNamara
Editor: Fletcher Doyle
Copy Editor: Nathan Heidelberger
Associate Art Director: Amy Greenan
Designer: Stephanie Flecha
Production Coordinator: Karol Szymczuk
Photo Research: J8 Media

The photographs in this book are used by permission and through the courtesy of:
Cover (left) Paul Souders/Corbis Documentary/Getty Images; cover (right) Amith Nag Photography/Moment/Getty Images; p. 4 tenra/iStock; p. 6 Darlyne A. Murawski/National Geographic/Getty Images; p. 7 Nancy Nehring/iStock; p. 8 IntergalacticDesignStudio/iStock; p. 10 Sari ONeal/Shutterstock.com; p. 11 (top) Alen Thien/Shutterstock.com; p. 11 (bottom) Brian Lasenby/Shutterstock.com; p. 16 furryclown/Shutterstock.com; p. 12 Aksenova Natalya/Shutterstock.com; p. 14 &#169 Lion Hijmans/iStock; p. 15 BlueRingMedia/Shutterstock.com; p. 17 Simon Shim/Shutterstock.com; p. 18 Stephen J. Krasemann/All Canada Photos/Getty Images; p. 19 Ingo Arndt/Nature Picture Library/Alamy Stock Photo; p. 20 (top) Arturo Pena Romano Medina/iStock/Thinkstock; p. 20 (bottom) Ian Redding/iStock/Thinkstock; p. 22 (left) Valentin Valkov/Shutterstock.com; p. 22 (right) File:Ant Mimic Spider.jpg/Shyamal/Wikimedia Commons; p. 24 Inventori/iStock/Thinkstock; p. 26 Morley Read/Alamy Stock Photo; p. 27 (top) London Scientific Films/Oxford Scientific/Getty Images; p. 27 (bottom) Ivan Kuzmin/Alamy Stock Photo.

Printed in the United States of America

Contents

"Arthropod" means "jointed foot," such as the joints in this grasshopper's legs.

Introduction: Count the Legs

When most people see a little creature with a lot of legs, they call it an **insect**. However, there are many kinds of six- or eight-legged creepy-crawlies. Insects and **arachnids** are both a kind of **arthropod**. So are crustaceans such as crabs, lobsters, and shrimp.

"Arthropod" means "jointed foot." All animals in the arthropod group have jointed legs. They are **invertebrates**, which means they don't have a backbone. Instead, they have a hard shell outside their body called

Insects and arachnids are important to the environment. This bee is pollinating flowers.

an **exoskeleton**. They have to shed this hard shell in order to grow.

There are a lot of insects and arachnids. More than one million species of insects have already been discovered. Scientists think there might be millions more insect species to be found. There are about sixty thousand known species of arachnids, and many more yet to be discovered.

Spiders—a type of arachnid—catch many insects in their webs.

Insects and arachnids are a valuable part of the **ecosystem**. Many insects, such as bees, flies, and butterflies, pollinate plants. Without them helping plants reproduce, none of our food could grow. Many animals eat insects. Some helpful arachnids and insects keep dangerous insects under control. If you have a spider in your house, you won't have as many insect pests.

Insects and arachnids are unique groups within the arthropod **phylum**. A phylum is a large group of related animals or plants. Though they share many characteristics, they also have many differences.

Some insects, such as these cockroaches, like to live in people's houses.

1 Easy to Find

nsects and arachnids are all around, both in wild places and probably in your house.

Some insects are very visible. If you go to a garden, you will probably see brightly colored butterflies visiting flowers. Bees will be buzzing there, too. Nearby, you might see a large pile of dirt with one or several holes in it—a sign of an ant **colony**.

Other insects are much harder to find. Some, like the walking stick, are common but blend into their environment so well that most

Butterflies are some of the most commonly seen insects.

people don't see them. Others, like the tiny fairyfly, are less than 0.04 inches (1 millimeter) long. A few, such as cicadas, live underground for more than a decade, then emerge for just a few days or weeks.

Arachnids are everywhere, too. Spiders are the most commonly seen arachnids. Like insects, they also live in woods, gardens, and houses, as well as in harsh environments like deserts. If you walk around the outside of your house or go to a local park, you will probably find a spider web. Spiders use the sticky web mostly to catch their food.

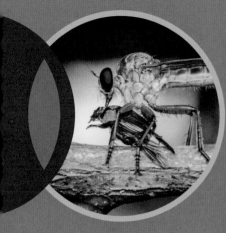

Zoom In

Some people call all insects and spiders "bugs." However, bugs are actually a very specific group of insects. True bugs are recognized by their sucking mouth-parts that look like a straw with a sharp pointed end.

Walking sticks are large insects, but they are hard to see because they look like the twigs they live among.

Arachnids include spiders, scorpions, daddy longlegs, mites, and blood-sucking ticks such as the one pictured.

2 Different Shapes

Though at first glance insects and arachnids may look similar, they are really very different. The most familiar kinds of arachnids are spiders. They range in size from tiny house spiders that are probably lurking in your room right now, to the huge Goliath bird-eating tarantula, which can get up to 11 inches (28 centimeters) long and weigh 6 ounces (170 grams). Scorpions, ticks, mites, and daddy longlegs are also kinds of arachnids.

All arachnids have eight legs. Spiders also have two more structures that, in some

Spiders have extra body parts near their mouths that sometimes look like extra legs—though they have only eight actual legs.

cases, look like extra legs. These are in the front of their bodies and are used to help in feeding and defense.

Two Sections

Arachnid bodies are divided into two segments: the **cephalothorax** (front half) and the **abdomen** (belly.) Unlike many insects, arachnids don't ever have wings or **antennae**. Spiders have several pairs of simple eyes.

Spider Anatomy

leg

palp

chelicera

spinneret

abdomen   cephalothorax

Arachnids have eight legs, two palps for feeding, and two body segments.

Insects have six legs. Their bodies are divided into three segments: head, **thorax**, and abdomen. Many— though not all—insects have wings. All insects have a pair of antennae on their heads. Antennae are sensory organs. Exactly what they sense varies from species to species. Some are mainly about touch, or feeling heat or vibrations. They can help an insect find its way

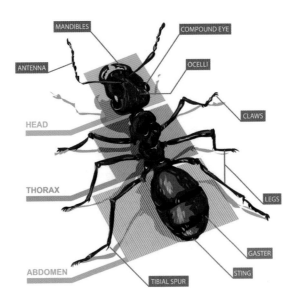

The three sections of an insect's body—the head, the thorax, and the abdomen—are easily seen on an ant.

around or sense approaching danger. In some insects, the antennae are used to detect chemicals in the air. Moths, for example, have big feathery antennae that can help them track down food or mates. Some males can sense the chemicals from female moths from miles away.

Insects and arachnids are different in ways other than their body forms. All spiders and most arachnids are predatory. In other words, they hunt other animals for food. Most eat insects, but some eat other arachnids.

Insects and Arachnids Explained

Spiders and scorpions inject a venom that liquefies their prey.

A few of the largest spiders can even eat very small birds or mammals, but this is unusual. Spiders inject their prey with a venom that dissolves their insides. Then the spider can suck up liquid food.

Varied Diet

Insects have a wider variety of feeding habits. Some are predatory. Many others eat plants. Some, like butterflies and moths, suck nectar from flowers. Insects such as

Many insects, such as butterflies and moths, undergo metamorphosis.

mosquitoes and ticks need a blood meal from an animal in order to reproduce.

Most arachnids and insects hatch from eggs. There are a few species in each group whose eggs hatch inside the female's body. Then she gives birth to live young. This is the case with scorpions and with some cockroaches.

Once born, insects and arachnids often develop differently. In arachnids, and some insects, the babies look like tiny versions of the adults. They shed their exoskeletons (molt) as they grow bigger. However, some insects, such as butterflies, undergo **metamorphosis**.

Zoom In

There are a few kinds of spiders that hunt fish. They anchor their hind legs on the dry land and grab small fish with their front legs.

This means that the baby form is completely different than the adult form. Butterflies begin as caterpillars, which then form a cocoon. Inside the cocoon, the caterpillar's body actually dissolves, then reshapes into a butterfly.

1. Tarantulas look scary, but they usually don't bite, and with proper care they can make good pets.

2. Some insects feed on plant life.

3 8 Be an Insect/Arachnid Detective

1. You find a creature under your bed. You see it has eight legs and two distinct body sections. Is it an insect or an arachnid?

2. You find an animal with six legs and three distinct body segments. It has antennae on its head. When you try to catch it, it flies away. Is it an insect or an arachnid?

3. Your teacher gives you a small egg to hatch. When the baby emerges, it looks like a worm or grub. Later, it spins a

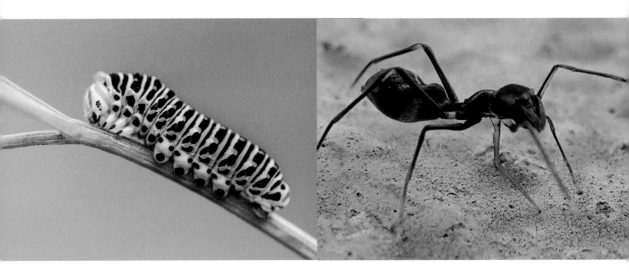

3. The juvenile butterfly (*left*)—known as a caterpillar—looks very different from an adult butterfly.

4. Some animals mimic—or look a lot like—other animals. This spider looks very much like an ant, and hides its extra pair of legs.

cocoon. When it emerges, it looks completely different, with brightly colored wings. Is this an insect or an arachnid? What is the name for the process by which it changed its form as it got older?

4. You see an animal that at first looks like a large ant. However, when you look at it more closely you see that it actually has eight legs. Is it an insect or an arachnid?

Insects and Arachnids Explained

Answer Key

1. It is an arachnid. Arachnids have eight legs and two body segments. Insects have six legs and three body segments.

2. It is an insect. Only insects have six legs and three body segments. No arachnid has antennae or wings.

3. The animal is an insect because it went through metamorphosis, or the process by which insects change from one form to another as they mature.

4. If it has eight legs, it is an arachnid. Some spiders mimic (look like) ants, but if you look closely, you can see that they are arachnids, not insects.

Bees live together in a community where every member works for the good of the group.

Rule Breakers

Many kinds of insects are known for living in large groups. Insects such as ants and bees have a queen that is the mother of most of the colony. Every member of the colony has a job to do, and they work together to keep the colony alive. They take care of the babies until they are grown. Most arachnids, on the other hand, are solitary. That means they live alone.

A few arachnids, however, have social lives. There are some spider species that build communal webs. They live together and even cooperate in catching food, which they then

A few kinds of spiders live in groups on the same web, hunting together and sharing meals.

share. Some species raise all of their babies together. Sometimes, only a few females reproduce, while the others just help take care of the offspring.

Another type of arachnid, the scorpion, is usually solitary. However, mother scorpions take excellent care of their children, called scorplings. They carry them on their back and care for them through their first molt.

Scorpions usually live alone, and often fight other scorpions.

Though usually solitary, scorpions are good mothers and carry their babies on their backs, protecting them until they are big enough to be on their own.

abdomen The rear part of an insect or arthropod body, containing the digestive system.

antennae The long sensory organs on the heads of insects and crustaceans.

arachnid An arthropod with eight legs and two body segments.

arthropod An invertebrate animal with jointed legs and an exoskeleton.

cephalothorax A joined head and thorax, the first segment of an arachnid.

colony A group of organisms living and working together for the benefit of the group.

ecosystem A community of organisms and the environment they live in.

exoskeleton The hard external body covering of some invertebrates, such as insects and arachnids.

insect An arthropod with six legs, three body segments, and antennae.

invertebrate An animal that doesn't have a spinal column, which is the backbone.

metamorphosis The process by which an insect changes from juvenile to adult, showing very different forms at each stage.

phylum A large group of plants or animals. In the seven levels of the ranking system called taxonomy, phylum is below kingdom and above class.

thorax The middle of three insect body segments, where legs and wings are attached.

Find Out More

Books

Johnson, Jinny. *Simon & Schuster Children's Guide to Insects and Spiders*. New York: Simon & Schuster Books for Young Readers, 1997.

Mound, Laurence. *Insect*. DK Eyewitness Books. New York: DK Publishing, 2007.

Murawski, Darlyne. *Ultimate Bugopedia: The Most Complete Bug Reference Ever*. Washington, DC: National Geographic Kids, 2013.

Sill, Cathryn. *About Arachnids: A Guide for Children*. Atlanta, GA: Peachtree Publishers, 2006.

Websites

Ducksters: Bugs (Insects and Arachnids)
http://www.ducksters.com/animals/bugs.php
This site gives an overview of the differences between insects and arachnids, and has some fun facts.

Easy Science for Kids
http://easyscienceforkids.com/animals/insects
On this site you can find links to many pages about insects, arachnids, and other interesting invertebrates.

Index

Page numbers in **boldface** are illustrations.

Laura L. Sullivan is the author of more than thirty fiction and nonfiction books for children, including the fantasies *Under the Green Hill* and *Guardian of the Green Hill*. She has written many books for Cavendish Square, including three titles in the Distinctions in Nature series.